T0417930

MYTHOLOGY OF THE WORLD

GODS OF WORLD MYTHOLOGY

by Pam Watts

BrightP★int Press

San Diego, CA

© 2023 BrightPoint Press
an imprint of ReferencePoint Press, Inc.
Printed in the United States

For more information, contact:
BrightPoint Press
PO Box 27779
San Diego, CA 92198
www.BrightPointPress.com

LIBRARY OF CONGRESS CATALOGING-IN-PUBLICATION DATA

Name: Watts, Pam, author.
Title: Gods of World Mythology / by Pam Watts.
Description: San Diego, CA: BrightPoint Press, 2023 | Series: Mythology of the World |
   Includes bibliographical references and index. | Audience: Grades 7–9
Identifiers: ISBN 9781678204921 (hardcover) | ISBN 9781678204938 (eBook)
The complete Library of Congress record is available at www.loc.gov.

CONTENTS

AT A GLANCE

- Myths are stories people have told to explain how they believe the world works.

- Many gods show people how to live their lives.

- There are many types of gods, including ruler gods, wisdom gods, gods of change and war, and gods of the underworld.

- Ruler gods explain how the world is organized.

- Wisdom gods help mankind find meaning and grow.

- Gods of change and war provide obstacles to overcome.

- Some myths show that hardship is often needed for growth.

- Gods of the underworld help humans transition from life to death.

- In some underworld myths, death is the end of one journey and the beginning of another.

INTRODUCTION

WHAT IS A GOD?

In the beginning, there was only ocean. Then the sun god Ra woke himself into being. He set order to the world. He blew over the waters and created Sky. He lifted Earth from the deep.

Earth and Sky had four children. Their sons were Osiris and Seth. Their daughters were Isis and Nephthys (NEF-this). Osiris married Isis, and Seth married Nephthys.

Osiris was special. Ra created Osiris out of himself. He made Osiris to rule the world.

One night, Osiris mistook Nephthys for Isis. He had a child with her. The child's name was Anubis. Seth was outraged.

Isis, Ra, Osiris, and Anubis (left to right) were key figures in many Egyptian myths. Osiris became the god of the underworld.

ISIS   RA   OSIRIS   ANUBIS

He killed Osiris. He then sliced Osiris into pieces. He tossed the pieces into the Nile River.

Isis discovered what had happened. She transformed into a bird. She flew over Egypt crying. She collected the pieces of Osiris's body. She then fanned them with her feathers. The wind drew out Osiris's spirit. She swallowed the spirit and gave birth to Horus. Horus trained as a warrior. He then killed Seth to **avenge** his father.

Osiris's death was not the end of his story. Isis, Nephthys, and Anubis got together with Thoth, the god of wisdom.

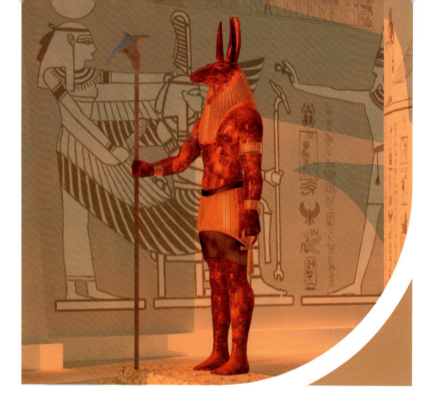

Many ancient Egyptians pictured Seth with a jackal-like head. This god is known for killing his brother in a burst of anger.

They put the pieces of Osiris back together. He was the first mummy. Isis spoke magic words over his body.

Osiris's soul was reborn in the underworld. He became the judge of all who die. Thoth recorded Osiris's judgments.

Anubis transformed into a jackal. He guided the newly dead to the underworld.

WHAT IS A MYTH?

This story is a myth from ancient Egypt. Writer Joseph Campbell spent his life studying myths. He said, "It has always been the prime function of mythology . . . to supply the **symbols** that carry the human spirit forward."[1] Myths give people new ways to think about their lives. They help people explore important topics. Many myths tell stories about gods. There have been thousands of gods.

Myths helped ancient cultures understand important topics. The gods featured in these stories helped guide people's lives.

They are as different as the people who have worshipped them. Gods represent divine action and purpose.

Certain types of gods appear across **polytheistic** religions. There are ruler gods, wisdom gods, and warring gods. There are also gods of death and rebirth.

1
GODS WHO RULE THE LIVING WORLD

Nearly every mythology has a ruling god. He creates order and passes judgment. The other gods see him as a king. They must follow his orders. Sometimes another god replaces the ruling god. Either he retires or another god overthrows him. Nature-based religions often consider the sun to be the ruling god.

SUN GODS

Myths answer questions people have about the world. But they also reflect the people who made them. The ancient Egyptians

Nature plays a big part in many myths. A sun god is the ruling god in many mythologies.

were farmers. Nature ordered their lives.

The Nile River flooded every year. This

made the earth fertile for crops. The sun

started and ended people's days. Ra was

their sun god.

A different Egyptian creation myth starts

with a lotus flower. It was alone. The flower

bloomed. Ra peeked from its petals. He

was the first light in the world. Then a bennu

bird sang. It was the first sound. The rest of

creation followed.

People saw Ra as the sun itself. They

said Ra rose and set with the sun's

movements. This cycle continued every

The bennu in Egyptian mythology was a large bird.
It is believed to have looked like a heron.

day. A scarab beetle lifted him from the underworld in the morning. Ra then steered a sun boat to the top of the heavens. In the afternoon, he became a falcon. He drifted to the horizon. He sailed back to the underworld each night.

The Inca also worshipped the sun. They called it Inti. They believed a greater

THE END OF AN EMPIRE

In 1526, the Inca saw a buzzard attack an eagle. The eagle fell to the earth during a festival for Inti. This event foretold the fall of the Inca Empire. Spanish soldiers soon arrived in South America. They brought smallpox with them. This disease killed many people. The Spanish conquered the Inca within a few years.

unknowable god created the Earth. But he left Inti to rule the world.

The Inca believed the first people lived like animals. Inti watched them from the heavens. He was sad. He sent his children to Earth to teach the people useful skills. Inti's children came to Earth through a window in a mountain near Lake Titicaca. Inti gave his favorite son a golden rod. He told him to plant it whenever he rested. Inti said his children should settle where the rod sunk all the way into the ground. They finally found the place. They called it Cuzco, which means "the world's navel."

The Inca gathered around Inti's children. Inti's children taught men how to plant and make weapons. They taught women how to spin, weave, cook, and sew. These people then taught others. Civilization was born.

KING OF THE GODS

Other cultures had king-like gods who ruled over the other gods. Odin, from Norse mythology, was this type of god. Giants gave birth to Odin and his two brothers. The giants then left them in a vast emptiness surrounded by fire and mist. To make the world, Odin and his brothers slew the first

Odin became the Norse god of war. He was also known as the protector of heroes.

giant. His blood formed the sea. His skull

formed the sky. His brains made clouds.

And his bones became hills.

To make humans, Odin and his brothers

found two stumps. One was from an ash

tree. One was from an elm. Odin blew life

into them. His brothers then gave humans minds and senses. The brothers carved one woman and named her Embla. They carved one man and named him Ask.

But creation was not enough for Odin. He cut out one of his eyes to pay for wisdom. To gain magical power, he hung

TERRIFYING FIGURES IN GREEK MYTHOLOGY

Earth and Sky had monstrous children. The Cyclopes towered over mountains. Each had just one giant eye. The Furies had snakes for hair and cried blood. The Titans were also fearsome. The Titan Cronus ate his first five children. But his Titan wife tricked him. She replaced his sixth child, Zeus, with a stone.

himself from the world-tree, Yggdrasil.

For nine nights, he did not eat or drink.

His body was tossed by the wind. He was

near death.

He then looked down and saw the

words of power. He discovered he could

read them. In reading them, he gained their

power. His ropes broke. He was free.

There are many accounts of gods

creating the world. Edith Hamilton was a

famous collector of Greek myths. She said,

"The universe created the gods."[2] In Greek

mythology, Earth and Sky created gods

Every day for many years, Prometheus suffered a horrible death. His suffering did not end until Hercules rescued him.

called Titans. Cronus was their leader. He

ruled until his son Zeus overthrew him.

Prometheus was another Titan. He

fought alongside Zeus in the war against

Cronus. In exchange for Prometheus's help, Zeus let him create humans.

Prometheus made humans walk upright like gods. He also made them intelligent. And he gave them the gods' fire to protect themselves.

When Zeus saw how godlike humans were, he was furious. Zeus strapped Prometheus to a mountain. Every day an eagle killed Prometheus by eating his liver. He then would be reborn. Prometheus suffered for many years. Finally, the hero Hercules took pity on him. Hercules killed the eagle and rescued Prometheus.

2

GODS WHO INSPIRE

Societies need structure. But people also want meaning and purpose. They like to create. The inspiration gods help them. These are the gods of learning and wisdom. They teach humans to become better people.

GODS OF LEARNING AND WISDOM

Quetzalcóatl (KET-sahl-KOH-ah-tul) is the Aztec god of wisdom. The Aztecs believed the world was created and destroyed many times. A giant flood once killed all humans. Quetzalcóatl traveled to the underworld to gather their bones.

The Quetzalcóatl Pyramid in Mexico shows the head of the Aztec god of wisdom. Quetzalcóatl used his wisdom to outsmart the king of the dead.

The king of the dead did not want to give them up. He told Quetzalcóatl he could have the bones if he played the king's trumpet. This was a trick. The trumpet was a conch shell with no holes.

History professor Mark Cartwright wrote, "The clever Quetzalcóatl gets around the problem by having worms drill holes in the conch and putting bees inside to make it sound."[3] Quetzalcóatl's success meant he was able to take the bones and return them to Earth. The gods ground them into dust and bled on them. The bones became new humans.

Väinämöinen wanted Aino to become his wife. But she had other plans.

The Finnish hero Väinämöinen (vine-uh-MOY-nen) stayed in his mother's womb for 730 years. During that time, she created the world. According to Finland's epic poem the *Kalevala*, Väinämöinen got tired of living "in a resting-place so gloomy, in a dwelling far too narrow."[4] He forced himself from his mother's womb. He fell into the ocean. He floated for eight years before finding land.

Väinämöinen is the basis for the wizard **archetype**. He was known for his magical wisdom. It allowed him to travel to Manala. This was the Finnish realm of the dead.

Väinämöinen was also famous for his beautiful songs. A young musician named Joukahainen (YOU-ka-hi-nen) became jealous. He challenged Väinämöinen to a singing contest. Väinämöinen easily won. Joukahainen then challenged him to a

A statue of Väinämöinen stands in downtown Helsinki. The Finnish hero was said to sing magical songs that enchanted all who heard them.

physical battle. This angered Väinämöinen.

He sang a song to magically raise up a

swamp to swallow Joukahainen. It would

have. But Joukahainen offered Väinämöinen his sister Aino for a wife.

Aino was upset. She did not want to marry such an old man. She threw herself in the ocean. Väinämöinen was out fishing and caught a salmon. When he started to cut it open, the fish stopped him. The salmon said she was Aino. She swam away. He searched for years. But he never found Aino again.

GODS OF ARTISTS AND CRAFTSMEN

The Tuatha Dé Danann (THOO-a DAY DU-non) of Ireland had many gods of learning.

The Dagda's wisdom helped him after the Formorians stole his magical harp. He was able to get it back with the help of Ogma and Lugh.

The Dagda was the chief god of the Tuatha

Dé Danann. He was the god of wisdom.

The god Ogma invented writing. With it he

created music, poetry, and spellcasting. Lugh was the god of craftsmen.

The Tuatha Dé Danann were at war with the Formorians. The Dagda had a magical harp. He played it to give his people courage when they rode into battle. During a battle the Formorians stole the Dagda's harp. Ogma and Lugh offered to help him get it back.

They journeyed to the Formorian castle. The harp was hanging on the wall. But warriors guarded it. The Dagda stretched out his hand. The harp sprang to him.

Lugh told the Dagda to play the chord of laughter. The Formorians laughed. Ogma told the Dagda to play the chord of grief. The Formorians wept. But each time the music stopped, they became furious.

Then the Dagda played the chord of sleep. The Formorians drifted back down. The gods tiptoed away.

THE ORIGINS OF FAIRIES

The Tuatha Dé Danann were a tribe of humans born of the gods. They were defeated by a tribe of humans called the Milesians. Afterward, each tribe agreed to rule half of Ireland. The Milesians took the aboveground half. The Tuatha Dé Danann retreated beneath the ground and became fairies.

3

GODS WHO MEDDLE

The inspiration gods encourage growth. But life is not always about moving forward. Sometimes it is about changes and endings. There are gods for these things, too. They are the gods of **chaos** and war. Seth was a god of chaos in

Egyptian mythology. Horus, who killed him, was a god of war.

Gods of chaos and war make problems that others must overcome. But in a way, these gods are needed. Humans would avoid many struggles if they could. But struggles can help people grow.

Ancient Egyptians carved falcon-headed statues of Horus and put them at temples, such as the Temple of Edfu.

Loki caused his share of trouble in Norse mythology. Many of the other gods feared the children he had with a giantess.

GODS OF CHAOS

Trickster gods like the Norse god Loki

threaten order. Loki never fit in. He got into

mischief and caused trouble. But he also

saved the gods often. Loki was friendly with

giants whom the other gods feared. Loki

married a goddess. But he also sneaked off and had three children with a giantess.

The gods were afraid of Loki's children. The first was a giant snake. Odin sent him to the sea. Loki's daughter was a beautiful maiden on one side. But on the other side, she was a **corpse**. Odin sent her to rule over the dead.

Loki's last child was the wolf Fenrir. He was huge and strong. Odin dreamed Fenrir would destroy the gods. Odin decided to trick him. He pretended to test his strength. He trapped Fenrir in magical bindings the wolf could not break.

Odin created a plan to keep Fenrir from destroying the Norse gods. He tricked the large wolf into being tied up in magical ropes.

In a retelling by fantasy writer Neil Gaiman, Fenrir said, "If you had not lied to me, I would have been a friend to the gods. But your fear has betrayed you. . . . I will eat the sun and I will eat the moon. But I will take the most pleasure in killing you."[5]

Every journey involves at least one transition. The Roman god Janus is a symbol of this type of change. He represents beginnings and endings. Janus is known as the two-faced god. He has a face on both sides of his head.

Not much is known about Janus. Most Roman gods have a Greek twin. But Janus does not. His image is placed above doorways and on bridges. According to the popular writer Rick Riordan, "The god of doorways has two faces, looking forward and backward, in and out."[6]

Some myths say that in the early days of the Roman Empire, Rome was attacked. The enemy tried to climb the walls of the

The two-faced Roman god Janus has become a symbol of beginnings and endings. The month of January was named for him.

city. Janus sprayed the attackers with

boiling water. They were forced to retreat.

From then on, the doors to Janus's temple

were always left open during war so he

could help.

GODS OF WAR

War gods are common to nearly every culture. War has helped societies throughout history grow. It has also destroyed many of them.

Nergal was the Mesopotamian god of war. He was lying in bed one day, bored. His weapons lined the wall. They began badgering him. They said he used to make the oceans boil. But now he was as weak as a child. The humans mocked him.

Nergal called his seven fiercest warriors. They were already in a fighting mood. The warriors said there were too many people in

Babylon. They thought these people ate all the food and made too much noise. Nergal and his warriors rode out spreading terror. They set fire to Babylon. They killed all its people.

Nergal was so fierce he drove out the other gods. The world was in chaos. Ishum, the god of fire, stepped in. Ishum was Nergal's friend. But he waged war against Nergal to save the world. Nergal finally saw what he had done. He stopped. Order was restored.

In ancient Slavic mythology, violence is seen as a cycle that never ends. Perun

The Mesopotamian god Nergal enjoyed fighting and destroying everything around him. Myths about Nergal helped people understand why suffering existed.

was the Slavic god of war. He was also the king of the living. Veles was king of the dead. He was a giant serpent. He carried Perun's wife away to the underworld. Veles became Perun's mortal enemy. They were in constant war.

The constant fighting between Perun (pictured)and Veles represents the cycles between order and war, and between life and death. Each time the fighting stopped, it always began again.

Once, Veles slithered to the top of the

world tree. He stopped the water of life

from flowing. The world began dying. Perun

came with his mighty axe and chopped

Veles into pieces. Then the waters ran

free. Perun celebrated with a mighty crash

of thunder.

But death never lasted. Veles was

continually reborn only to find himself in

conflict with Perun repeatedly. The cycle of

war never ended.

THE BALANCE OF LIFE AND DEATH

The cycle of war between Perun and Veles was a symbol of the balance of life and death. Perun ruled the living world while Veles ruled the afterlife. Like life and death, neither Perun nor Veles could exist without the other.

4

GODS WHO RULE THE UNDERWORLD

Death is part of life. But in myths death is not always the end. Some gods help people move from life into death. For example, gods or beings known as psychopomps (SAHY-koh-pomps) guide souls to the underworld. Anubis is this type of god. Rulers such as Osiris watch over the

souls once they arrive.

SPIRIT GUIDES

A Breton myth states that the last person

who dies on New Year's Eve becomes

the god Ankou. He collects the souls of all

Anubis is often shown with the head of a jackal. But this Egyptian god has the body of a human.

those who die the next year. He comes as a skeleton. He drives a wooden cart with two skeleton helpers. If someone hears a cart creaking, his time on this earth is over. The Ankou is released on the next New Year's Day when a new Ankou takes his place.

In many myths, the spirit guide drives a boat. He transports souls across a river to the land of the dead. Ursanabi is the Mesopotamian spirit guide. He appears in the poem the *Epic of Gilgamesh*.

The gods created Gilgamesh to be the perfect hero. But he was so powerful he frightened them. They made Enkidu to

Sometimes the Ankou is depicted as a plain skeleton. Other times he is shown with long white hair and a hat.

challenge him. Enkidu became Gilgamesh's dearest friend instead.

Enkidu had a dream. In the poem, he wakes and says to Gilgamesh, "Among the dead I shall sit. The threshold of the dead

I shall cross. Never again shall I set eyes on my dear brother."[7] Then, Enkidu fell ill and died. Gilgamesh was heartbroken. He decided to bring Enkidu back.

A sorceress told Gilgamesh to seek Ursanabi beside the waters of death. He agreed to take Gilgamesh across the waters to the land of the dead. The king

EPICS

An epic is a long poem about heroes. Most epics were passed down through storytellers. First recorded more than 4,000 years ago, the *Epic of Gilgamesh* is one of the oldest stories of this kind. The loyal and determined Gilgamesh becomes a hero when he risks his life for the sake of others.

of the underworld told Gilgamesh about a plant that could bring someone back from the dead. But it grew at the bottom of the waters of death.

Gilgamesh refused to give up. So Ursanabi agreed to take him. Gilgamesh tied stones to his feet and dove into the water. He found the plant and plucked it. Although it wounded him, he held tight. He cut off the stones and shot back to the surface.

He and Ursanabi returned to land. Gilgamesh fell asleep. While he slept, a serpent ate the plant. It gave the animal the

In 1853, a clay tablet was found in the Middle East. A part of the Epic of Gilgamesh poem appears on it.

power to stay young. The serpent robbed Gilgamesh of his chance to bring Enkidu back to life.

KINGS OF THE DEAD

Some cultures fear the underworld. The kings of these places are often scary and evil. In Mongolian and Hungarian mythology,

Erlik Khan and Ulgen were brothers.

Ulgen was given the task of creation. Erlik

was jealous.

Ulgen crafted humans from mud. He set

a black dog to watch over them. He then

took a nap. It was cold and snowing. Erlik

lured the dog away with a fur coat. With the

dog gone, Erlik spat on the humans. This

act is why humans have pain and disease.

As punishment, Erlik was sent to the

underworld. He created demons to further

trouble humans.

Other underworlds are places of growth,

healing, and transition. The *Mabinogion* is

Arawn saw Pwyll chase the pack of dogs away from the giant stag. Pwyll then took Arawn's place in Annwfn to earn his forgiveness.

an ancient book of myths from Wales. It

tells of a prince named Pwyll (POOL) who

was hunting in the woods with his pack of

dogs. In a clearing, another pack of dogs

attacked a giant stag.

The dogs were bright white. Their ears were blood red. Pwyll chased them away. His pack claimed the stag.

A mighty horseman approached Pwyll. He asked why Pwyll had claimed the kill. The horseman told Pwyll he was Arawn, the king of Annwfn.

Pwyll was afraid. Annwfn was the land of the dead. The *Mabinogion* states that Pwyll then asked the king, "How shall I win your friendship?"[8]

Arawn smiled. He had a rival in Annwfn. He would forgive Pwyll on one condition. Arawn wanted Pwyll to take his place in

Annwfn for a year and defeat Arawn's rival while Arawn stayed on Earth.

Pwyll took the form of Arawn and traveled to Annwfn. Arawn's enemy tried to trick Pwyll. But Pwyll did not fall for the trick. He defeated the enemy and became Arawn's friend.

Journeys to the underworld often help gods and heroes grow. Pwyll returned to the living world wiser than when he left. Gilgamesh was also changed by his time in the land of the dead.

Myths about gods are part of nearly every culture. They help explain both the

GODS OF WORLD MYTHOLOGY

Irish: Tuatha Dé Danann **Norse: Odin, Loki** **Finnish: Väinämöinen** **Greek: Zeus** **Mongolian: Erlik Khan, Ulgen**

Aztec: Quetzalcóatl **Inca: Inti** **Roman: Janus** **Egyptian: Anubis, Ra** **Mesopotamian: Gilgamesh, Nergal**

Each ancient culture had its own set of gods and myths that told the gods' stories.

world itself and humans' experiences in it.

For thousands of years, these stories have

helped people understand their own lives.

GLOSSARY

archetype
a type of character who appears in many stories across cultures

avenge
to get revenge on behalf of oneself or another person

chaos
disorder and confusion

corpse
a dead body

polytheistic
worshipping many gods

symbols
objects that represent ideas

SOURCE NOTES

INTRODUCTION: WHAT IS A GOD?

1. Joseph Campbell, *The Hero with a Thousand Faces*. Novato, CA: New World Library, 2008, p. 7.

CHAPTER ONE: GODS WHO RULE THE LIVING WORLD

2. Edith Hamilton, *Mythology*. New York: Black Dog & Leventhal Publishers, 2017, p. 17.

CHAPTER TWO: GODS WHO INSPIRE

3. Mark Cartwright, "Quetzalcóatl," *World History Encyclopedia*, August 1, 2013. www.worldhistory.org.

4. Quoted in Elias Lönnrot, W.F. Kirby, trans., *Kalevala: The Land of the Heroes* (Volume I). Project Gutenberg, 2008, eBook, Rune 1, Lines 297–8.

CHAPTER THREE: GODS WHO MEDDLE

5. Neil Gaiman, *Norse Mythology*. New York: W.W. Norton & Company, 2017, p. 106.

6. Rick Riordan, "The Month of Janus," *RickRiordan.com*, January 22, 2022. https://rickriordan.com.

CHAPTER FOUR: GODS WHO RULE THE UNDERWORLD

7. Quoted in Andrew George, trans., *The Epic of Gilgamesh*. New York: Penguin Books, 1999, eBook.

8. Quoted in Gwyn and Thomas Jones, trans., *The Mabinogion*. London: J.M. Dent & Sons, 1973, pp. 3–4.

FOR FURTHER RESEARCH

BOOKS

Rachel Bithell, *Goddesses of World Mythology*. San Diego, CA: BrightPoint Press, 2023.

Chris Penard, *Celtic Mythology for Kids: Tales of Selkies, Giants, and the Sea*. Berkeley, CA: Rockridge Press, 2020.

Marchella Ward, *The Met Gods of the Ancient World: A Kids' Guide to Ancient Mythologies, From Mayan to Norse, Egyptian to Yoruba*. New York: DK Children, 2022.

INTERNET SOURCES

"Ancient Egyptian Gods and Goddesses," *DK FindOut!*, 2022. www.dkfindout.com.

"The Gods and Goddesses of Ancient Greece!" *National Geographic Kids*, n.d. www.natgeokids.com.

"The Whole Interesting History of the Tuatha de Danann: Ireland's Most Ancient Race," *Connolly Cove*, May 14, 2022. www.connollycove.com.

WEBSITES

Discovering Ancient Egypt
https://discoveringegypt.com

This site includes stories about ancient Egyptian gods, as well as maps and drawings related to this civilization's mythology.

Greek Mythology
www.greekmythology.com

This site includes a set of stories about the gods, goddesses, and heroes of the ancient Greeks.

Mythopedia
https://mythopedia.com

This site includes information about myths from numerous civilizations of the world.

INDEX

IMAGE CREDITS

ABOUT THE AUTHOR

Pam Watts is a writer and teacher. She thinks a lot about the meaning of life. To understand it better, she has studied physics at Wellesley College and the classics at St. John's College. She also earned an MFA in Writing for Children & Young Adults from Vermont College of Fine Arts.